Wilson Language Basics

Composition Book

Level 2

SECOND EDITION

Wilson Language Training Corporation

www.wilsonlanguage.com

www.fundations.com

Fundations® Student Composition Book 2

Item # F2STCBK2

ISBN 978-1-56778-507-4

SECOND EDITION

PUBLISHED BY:

Wilson Language Training Corporation
47 Old Webster Road
Oxford, MA 01540
United States of America

(800) 899-8454

www.wilsonlanguage.com

Printed in the U.S.A.

December 2018

① Sit *right*

Seat pulled in, feet on floor

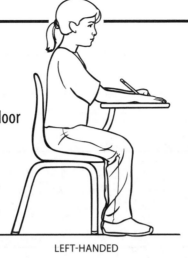 

LEFT-HANDED　　　　RIGHT-HANDED

② Place paper and hands *right*

Paper slanted, wrist straight, elbow on desk, other hand holding paper

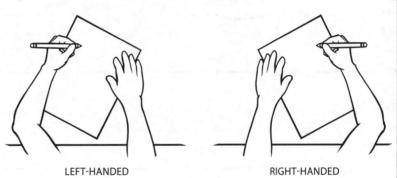

LEFT-HANDED　　　　RIGHT-HANDED

③ Grip pencil *right*

Pencil held between index finger and thumb, resting on the other fingers

LEFT-HANDED　　　　RIGHT-HANDED

Let's *write!*

Sounds

1 ank   2 am

3 ch   4 besk

Review Words

1 inch   2 sting

Current Words

1 dank   2

Trick Words

1   2

Sentences

1 The tank is fu

2 are you in that

fencla b

Sounds

1 fred   2

3 dzed   4

Review Words

1   2

Current Words

/t/   /t/
1 cheked   2 jumped

Trick Words

1   2

Sentences

1

2

Sounds

1 old   2 ing

3 ck / c / k   4 s / ss

Review Words

1 shrunk   2 napkin

Current Words

finish   2

Trick Words

1 Will m   2

Sentences

1 Will mom punish the

kids?

2

Wilson Fundations® | ©2003, 2012 Wilson Language Training

Sounds

1   2

3   4

Review Words

1   2

Current Words

1   2

Trick Words

1   2

Sentences

1

2

Sounds

1   2

3   4

Review Words

1   2

Current Words

1   2

Trick Words

1   2

Sentences

1

2

Sounds

1   2

3   4

Review Words

1   2

Current Words

1   2

Trick Words

1   2

Sentences

1

2

Sounds

1   2

3   4

Review Words

1   2

Current Words

1   2

Trick Words

1   2

Sentences

1

2

Wilson Fundations® | ©2003, 2012 Wilson Language Training Corporation

Sounds

1 _____ 2 _____

3 _____ 4 _____

Review Words

1 _____ 2 _____

Current Words

1 _____ 2 _____

Trick Words

1 _____ 2 _____

Sentences

1 _____

2 _____

Sounds

1 _____ 2 _____

3 _____ 4 _____

Review Words

1 _____ 2 _____

Current Words

1 _____ 2 _____

Trick Words

1 _____ 2 _____

Sentences

1 _____

2 _____

Sounds

1 _____ 2 _____

3 _____ 4 _____

Review Words

1 _____ 2 _____

Current Words

1 _____ 2 _____

Trick Words

1 _____ 2 _____

Sentences

1 _____

2 _____

Sounds

1   2

3   4

Review Words

1   2

Current Words

1   2

Trick Words

1   2

Sentences

1

2

Sounds

1   2

3   4

Review Words

1   2

Current Words

1   2

Trick Words

1   2

Sentences

1

2

Sounds

1   2

3   4

Review Words

1   2

Current Words

1   2

Trick Words

1   2

Sentences

1

2

Sounds

1 _____ 2 _____

3 _____ 4 _____

Review Words

1 _____ 2 _____

Current Words

1 _____ 2 _____

Trick Words

1 _____ 2 _____

Sentences

1 _____

_____

2 _____

_____

Sounds

1 _____   2 _____

3 _____   4 _____

Review Words

1 _____   2 _____

Current Words

1 _____   2 _____

Trick Words

1 _____   2 _____

Sentences

1 _____

2 _____

Sounds

1   2

3   4

Review Words

1   2

Current Words

1   2

Trick Words

1   2

Sentences

1

2

Sounds

1 _____ 2 _____

3 _____ 4 _____

Review Words

1 _____ 2 _____

Current Words

1 _____ 2 _____

Trick Words

1 _____ 2 _____

Sentences

1 _____

_____

2 _____

_____

Sounds

1   2

3   4

Review Words

1   2

Current Words

1   2

Trick Words

1   2

Sentences

1

2

Sounds

1   2

3   4

Review Words

1   2

Current Words

1   2

Trick Words

1   2

Sentences

1

2

Sounds

1 _____ 2 _____

3 _____ 4 _____

Review Words

1 _____ 2 _____

Current Words

1 _____ 2 _____

Trick Words

1 _____ 2 _____

Sentences

1 _____

_____

2 _____

_____

Sounds

1   2

3   4

Review Words

1   2

Current Words

1   2

Trick Words

1   2

Sentences

1

2

Sounds

1   2

3   4

Review Words

1   2

Current Words

1   2

Trick Words

1   2

Sentences

1

2

Sounds

1 _____ 2 _____

3 _____ 4 _____

Review Words

1 _____ 2 _____

Current Words

1 _____ 2 _____

Trick Words

1 _____ 2 _____

Sentences

1 _____

2 _____

Sounds

1 _____ 2 _____

3 _____ 4 _____

Review Words

1 _____ 2 _____

Current Words

1 _____ 2 _____

Trick Words

1 _____ 2 _____

Sentences

1 _____

2 _____

Sounds

1   2

3   4

Review Words

1   2

Current Words

1   2

Trick Words

1   2

Sentences

1

2

Sounds

1   2

3   4

Review Words

1   2

Current Words

1   2

Trick Words

1   2

Sentences

1

2

Sounds

1   2

3   4

Review Words

1   2

Current Words

1   2

Trick Words

1   2

Sentences

1

2

Sounds

1   2

3   4

Review Words

1   2

Current Words

1   2

Trick Words

1   2

Sentences

1

2

Sounds

1   2

3   4

Review Words

1   2

Current Words

1   2

Trick Words

1   2

Sentences

1

2

Sounds

1 _____   2 _____

3 _____   4 _____

Review Words

1 _____   2 _____

Current Words

1 _____   2 _____

Trick Words

1 _____   2 _____

Sentences

1 _____

2 _____

Sounds

1   2

3   4

Review Words

1   2

Current Words

1   2

Trick Words

1   2

Sentences

1

2

Sounds

1   2

3   4

Review Words

1   2

Current Words

1   2

Trick Words

1   2

Sentences

1

2

Sounds

1 _____ 2 _____

3 _____ 4 _____

Review Words

1 _____ 2 _____

Current Words

1 _____ 2 _____

Trick Words

1 _____ 2 _____

Sentences

1 _____

2 _____

Sounds

1   2

3   4

Review Words

1   2

Current Words

1   2

Trick Words

1   2

Sentences

1

2

Sounds

1   2

3   4

Review Words

1   2

Current Words

1   2

Trick Words

1   2

Sentences

1

2

Sounds

1 _____ 2 _____

3 _____ 4 _____

Review Words

1 _____ 2 _____

Current Words

1 _____ 2 _____

Trick Words

1 _____ 2 _____

Sentences

1 _____

2 _____

Sounds

1 _____   2 _____

3 _____   4 _____

Review Words

1 _____   2 _____

Current Words

1 _____   2 _____

Trick Words

1 _____   2 _____

Sentences

1 _____

2 _____

Sounds

1   2

3   4

Review Words

1   2

Current Words

1   2

Trick Words

1   2

Sentences

1

2

Sounds

1 _____ 2 _____

3 _____ 4 _____

Review Words

1 _____ 2 _____

Current Words

1 _____ 2 _____

Trick Words

1 _____ 2 _____

Sentences

1

2

Sounds

1   2

3   4

Review Words

1   2

Current Words

1   2

Trick Words

1   2

Sentences

1

2

Sounds

1   2

3   4

Review Words

1   2

Current Words

1   2

Trick Words

1   2

Sentences

1

2

Sounds

1   2

3   4

Review Words

1   2

Current Words

1   2

Trick Words

1   2

Sentences

1

2

Sounds

1   2

3   4

Review Words

1   2

Current Words

1   2

Trick Words

1   2

Sentences

1

2

Sounds

1 _____ 2 _____

3 _____ 4 _____

Review Words

1 _____ 2 _____

Current Words

1 _____ 2 _____

Trick Words

1 _____ 2 _____

Sentences

1 _____

2 _____

Sounds

1   2

3   4

Review Words

1   2

Current Words

1   2

Trick Words

1   2

Sentences

1

2

Sounds

1 _____ 2 _____

3 _____ 4 _____

Review Words

1 _____ 2 _____

Current Words

1 _____ 2 _____

Trick Words

1 _____ 2 _____

Sentences

1 _____

2 _____

Sounds

1   2

3   4

Review Words

1   2

Current Words

1   2

Trick Words

1   2

Sentences

1

2

Sounds

1   2

3   4

Review Words

1   2

Current Words

1   2

Trick Words

1   2

Sentences

1

2

Sounds

1   2

3   4

Review Words

1   2

Current Words

1   2

Trick Words

1   2

Sentences

1

2

Sounds

1   2

3   4

Review Words

1   2

Current Words

1   2

Trick Words

1   2

Sentences

1

2

Sounds

1   2

3   4

Review Words

1   2

Current Words

1   2

Trick Words

1   2

Sentences

1

2

Sounds

1   2

3   4

Review Words

1   2

Current Words

1   2

Trick Words

1   2

Sentences

1

2

Sounds

1   2

3   4

Review Words

1   2

Current Words

1   2

Trick Words

1   2

Sentences

1

2

Sounds

1 _____   2 _____

3 _____   4 _____

Review Words

1 _____   2 _____

Current Words

1 _____   2 _____

Trick Words

1 _____   2 _____

Sentences

1 _____

2 _____

Sounds

1   2

3   4

Review Words

1   2

Current Words

1   2

Trick Words

1   2

Sentences

1

2

Wilson Fundations® | ©2003, 2012 Wilson Language Training Corporation

Sounds

1 _____ 2 _____

3 _____ 4 _____

Review Words

1 _____ 2 _____

Current Words

1 _____ 2 _____

Trick Words

1 _____ 2 _____

Sentences

1 _____

2 _____

Sounds

1   2

3   4

Review Words

1   2

Current Words

1   2

Trick Words

1   2

Sentences

1

2

Sounds

1 _____ 2 _____

3 _____ 4 _____

Review Words

1 _____ 2 _____

Current Words

1 _____ 2 _____

Trick Words

1 _____ 2 _____

Sentences

1 _____

2 _____

Sounds

1   2

3   4

Review Words

1   2

Current Words

1   2

Trick Words

1   2

Sentences

1

2

Sounds

1   2

3   4

Review Words

1   2

Current Words

1   2

Trick Words

1   2

Sentences

1

2

Sounds

1   2

3   4

Review Words

1   2

Current Words

1   2

Trick Words

1   2

Sentences

1

2

Sounds

1   2

3   4

Review Words

1   2

Current Words

1   2

Trick Words

1   2

Sentences

1

2

Sounds

_____

1 _____   2 _____

_____

3 _____   4 _____

Review Words

_____

1 _____   2 _____

Current Words

_____

1 _____   2 _____

Trick Words

_____

1 _____   2 _____

Sentences

_____

1 _____

_____

_____

2 _____

_____

Sounds

1 _____ 2 _____

3 _____ 4 _____

Review Words

1 _____ 2 _____

Current Words

1 _____ 2 _____

Trick Words

1 _____ 2 _____

Sentences

1 _____

2 _____

Sounds

_____

- -

1 _____ 2 _____

_____

_____

- -

3 _____ 4 _____

_____

Review Words

_____

- -

1 _____ 2 _____

_____

Current Words

_____

- -

1 _____ 2 _____

_____

Trick Words

- -

1 _____ 2 _____

_____

Sentences

- -

1 _____

_____

_____

- -

2 _____

_____

_____

- -

_____

Sounds

1   2

3   4

Review Words

1   2

Current Words

1   2

Trick Words

1   2

Sentences

1

2

Sounds

1 _____   2 _____

3 _____   4 _____

Review Words

1 _____   2 _____

Current Words

1 _____   2 _____

Trick Words

1 _____   2 _____

Sentences

1

2

Sounds

1 _____ 2 _____

3 _____ 4 _____

Review Words

1 _____ 2 _____

Current Words

1 _____ 2 _____

Trick Words

1 _____ 2 _____

Sentences

1 _____

2 _____

Sounds

1 _____ 2 _____

3 _____ 4 _____

Review Words

1 _____ 2 _____

Current Words

1 _____ 2 _____

Trick Words

1 _____ 2 _____

Sentences

1 _____

2 _____

Sounds

1   2

3   4

Review Words

1   2

Current Words

1   2

Trick Words

1   2

Sentences

1

2

Sounds

1   2

3   4

Review Words

1   2

Current Words

1   2

Trick Words

1   2

Sentences

1

2

Sounds

1 _____ 2 _____

3 _____ 4 _____

Review Words

1 _____ 2 _____

Current Words

1 _____ 2 _____

Trick Words

1 _____ 2 _____

Sentences

1 _____

2 _____

Sounds

1   2

3   4

Review Words

1   2

Current Words

1   2

Trick Words

1   2

Sentences

1

2

Sounds

1 _____ 2 _____

3 _____ 4 _____

Review Words

1 _____ 2 _____

Current Words

1 _____ 2 _____

Trick Words

1 _____ 2 _____

Sentences

1 _____

2 _____

Sounds

1   2

3   4

Review Words

1   2

Current Words

1   2

Trick Words

1   2

Sentences

1

2

Sounds

1   2

3   4

Review Words

1   2

Current Words

1   2

Trick Words

1   2

Sentences

1

2

Sounds

1   2

3   4

Review Words

1   2

Current Words

1   2

Trick Words

1   2

Sentences

1

2

Sounds

1   2

Review Words

1   2

Current Words

1   2

Trick Words

1   2

Sentences

1

2

Sounds

1 _____ 2 _____

3 _____ 4 _____

Review Words

1 _____ 2 _____

Current Words

1 _____ 2 _____

Trick Words

1 _____ 2 _____

Sentences

1 _____

2 _____

Sounds

1   2

3   4

Review Words

1   2

Current Words

1   2

Trick Words

1   2

Sentences

1

2

Sounds

1   2

3   4

Review Words

1   2

Current Words

1   2

Trick Words

1   2

Sentences

1

2

Sounds

1 _____   2 _____

3 _____   4 _____

Review Words

1 _____   2 _____

Current Words

1 _____   2 _____

Trick Words

1 _____   2 _____

Sentences

1 _____

2 _____

Sounds

1   2

3   4

Review Words

1   2

Current Words

1   2

Trick Words

1   2

Sentences

1

2

Sounds

1   2

3   4

Review Words

1   2

Current Words

1   2

Trick Words

1   2

Sentences

1

2

Sounds

1   2

3   4

Review Words

1   2

Current Words

1   2

Trick Words

1   2

Sentences

1

2

Sounds

1   2

3   4

Review Words

1   2

Current Words

1   2

Trick Words

1   2

Sentences

1

2

Sounds

1   2

3   4

5

Words

1   2

3   4

5

Trick Words

1   2

Sentences

_____ 1 _____

_____

_____

_____ 2 _____

_____

Unit Test Grading

Sounds: _____ / 5	Trick Words: _____ / 2		Score: _____	
Words: _____ / 5	Sentences:		x 4	
Marking: _____ / 5	Words: _____ / 5		Total Score: _____ / 100	
	Trick Words: _____ / 3			

☐ Legibility   ☐ Capitalization   ☐ Punctuation   ☐ Phrasing

Sounds

1 _____   2 _____

3 _____   4 _____

5 _____

Words

1 _____   2 _____

3 _____   4 _____

5 _____

Trick Words

1 _____   2 _____

Sentences

_____ 1 _____

_____

_____

_____ 2 _____

_____

Unit Test Grading

Sounds: _____ / 5	Trick Words: _____ / 2	Score: _____
Words: _____ / 5	Sentences:	x 4
Marking: _____ / 5	Words: _____ / 5	Total Score: _____ / 100
	Trick Words: _____ / 3	

☐ Legibility   ☐ Capitalization   ☐ Punctuation   ☐ Phrasing

Sounds

1 _____	2 _____

3 _____	4 _____

5 _____

Words

1 _____	2 _____

3 _____	4 _____

5 _____

Trick Words

1 _____	2 _____

Sentences

1

2

Unit Test Grading

Sounds: _____ / 5	Trick Words: _____ / 2	Score: _____	
Words: _____ / 5	Sentences:	x 4	
Marking: _____ / 5	Words: _____ / 5	Total Score: _____ / 100	
	Trick Words: _____ / 3		

☐ Legibility   ☐ Capitalization   ☐ Punctuation   ☐ Phrasing

Sounds

1 _____ 2 _____

3 _____ 4 _____

5 _____

Words

1 _____ 2 _____

3 _____ 4 _____

5 _____

Trick Words

1 _____ 2 _____

Sentences

_1 _____

_____

2 _____

_____

Unit Test Grading			
Sounds: _____ / 5	Trick Words: _____ / 2	Score: _____	
Words: _____ / 5	Sentences:	x 4	
Marking: _____ / 5	Words: _____ / 5	Total Score: _____ / 100	
	Trick Words: _____ / 3		

☐ Legibility   ☐ Capitalization   ☐ Punctuation   ☐ Phrasing

Sounds

1 _____ 2 _____

3 _____ 4 _____

5 _____

Words

1 _____ 2 _____

3 _____ 4 _____

5 _____

Trick Words

1 _____ 2 _____

Sentences

1 _____

_____

_____

2 _____

_____

_____

Unit Test Grading

Sounds: _____ / 5	Trick Words: _____ / 2		Score: _____	
Words: _____ / 5	Sentences:			x 4
Marking: _____ / 5	Words: _____ / 5		Total Score: _____ / 100	
	Trick Words: _____ / 3			

☐ Legibility   ☐ Capitalization   ☐ Punctuation   ☐ Phrasing

Sounds

1   2

3   4

5

Words

1   2

3   4

5

Trick Words

1   2

Sentences

1

2

Unit Test Grading

Sounds: _____ / 5	Trick Words: _____ / 2		Score: _____	
Words: _____ / 5	Sentences:			x 4
Marking: _____ / 5	Words: _____ / 5		Total Score: _____ / 100	
	Trick Words: _____ / 3			

☐ Legibility   ☐ Capitalization   ☐ Punctuation   ☐ Phrasing

Sounds

1 _____   2 _____

3 _____   4 _____

5 _____

Words

1 _____   2 _____

3 _____   4 _____

5 _____

Trick Words

1 _____   2 _____

Sentences

1 _____

_____

2 _____

_____

Unit Test Grading			
Sounds: _____ / 5	Trick Words: _____ / 2	Score: _____	
Words: _____ / 5	Sentences:	x 4	
Marking: _____ / 5	Words: _____ / 5	Total Score: _____ / 100	
	Trick Words: _____ / 3		

☐ Legibility   ☐ Capitalization   ☐ Punctuation   ☐ Phrasing

Sounds

1   2

3   4

5

Words

1   2

3   4

5

Trick Words

1   2

Sentences

_____
1 _____
_____

_____
_____
_____

_____
_____
_____

_____
2 _____
_____

_____
_____
_____

_____
_____
_____

Unit Test Grading

Sounds: _____ / 5	Trick Words: _____ / 2	Score: _____
Words: _____ / 5	Sentences:	x 4
Marking: _____ / 5	Words: _____ / 5	Total Score: _____ / 100
	Trick Words: _____ / 3	

☐ Legibility   ☐ Capitalization   ☐ Punctuation   ☐ Phrasing

Sounds

1 _____   2 _____

3 _____   4 _____

5 _____

Words

1 _____   2 _____

3 _____   4 _____

5 _____

Trick Words

1 _____   2 _____

Sentences

1 _____

_____

2 _____

_____

Unit Test Grading

Sounds: _____ / 5	Trick Words: _____ / 2		Score: _____	
Words: _____ / 5	Sentences:			x 4
Marking: _____ / 5	Words: _____ / 5		Total Score: _____ / 100	
	Trick Words: _____ / 3			

☐ Legibility   ☐ Capitalization   ☐ Punctuation   ☐ Phrasing

Sounds

1 _____   2 _____

3 _____   4 _____

5 _____

Words

1 _____   2 _____

3 _____   4 _____

5 _____

Trick Words

1 _____   2 _____

Sentences

1

2

Unit Test Grading

Sounds: _____ / 5	Trick Words: _____ / 2		Score: _____	
Words: _____ / 5	Sentences:		x 4	
Marking: _____ / 5	Words: _____ / 5		Total Score: _____ / 100	
	Trick Words: _____ / 3			

☐ Legibility   ☐ Capitalization   ☐ Punctuation   ☐ Phrasing

Sounds

1 _____   2 _____

3 _____   4 _____

5 _____

Words

1 _____   2 _____

3 _____   4 _____

5 _____

Trick Words

1 _____   2 _____

Sentences

_____

1 _____

_____

_____

_____

_____

2 _____

_____

_____

_____

_____

_____

Unit Test Grading

Sounds: _____ / 5	Trick Words: _____ / 2	Score: _____
Words: _____ / 5	Sentences:	x 4
Marking: _____ / 5	Words: _____ / 5	Total Score: _____ / 100
	Trick Words: _____ / 3	

☐ Legibility   ☐ Capitalization   ☐ Punctuation   ☐ Phrasing

Sounds

1 _____ 2 _____

3 _____ 4 _____

5 _____

Words

1 _____ 2 _____

3 _____ 4 _____

5 _____

Trick Words

1 _____ 2 _____

Sentences

1

2

Unit Test Grading

Sounds: _____ / 5	Trick Words: _____ / 2	Score: _____	
Words: _____ / 5	Sentences:	x 4	
Marking: _____ / 5	Words: _____ / 5	Total Score: _____ / 100	
	Trick Words: _____ / 3		

☐ Legibility   ☐ Capitalization   ☐ Punctuation   ☐ Phrasing

Sounds

1 _____   2 _____

3 _____   4 _____

5 _____

Words

1 _____   2 _____

3 _____   4 _____

5 _____

Trick Words

1 _____   2 _____

Sentences

1

2

<table>
<tr><td colspan="6" align="center">**Unit Test Grading**</td></tr>
<tr><td>Sounds:</td><td>_____ / 5</td><td>Trick Words:</td><td>_____ / 2</td><td>Score:</td><td>_____</td></tr>
<tr><td>Words:</td><td>_____ / 5</td><td>Sentences:</td><td></td><td></td><td>x 4</td></tr>
<tr><td>Marking:</td><td>_____ / 5</td><td>Words:</td><td>_____ / 5</td><td>Total Score:</td><td>_____ / 100</td></tr>
<tr><td></td><td></td><td>Trick Words:</td><td>_____ / 3</td><td></td><td></td></tr>
</table>

☐ Legibility   ☐ Capitalization   ☐ Punctuation   ☐ Phrasing

Sounds

1 _____   2 _____

3 _____   4 _____

5 _____

Words

1 _____   2 _____

3 _____   4 _____

5 _____

Trick Words

1 _____   2 _____

Sentences

_____
- -
1 _____
_____

_____
- -
_____
_____

_____
- -
_____
_____

_____
- -
2 _____
_____

_____
- -
_____
_____

_____
- -
_____
_____

Unit Test Grading

Sounds: _____ / 5	Trick Words: _____ / 2	Score: _____	
Words: _____ / 5	Sentences:	x 4	
Marking: _____ / 5	Words: _____ / 5	Total Score: _____ / 100	
	Trick Words: _____ / 3		

☐ Legibility   ☐ Capitalization   ☐ Punctuation   ☐ Phrasing

Sounds

1 _____ 2 _____

3 _____ 4 _____

5 _____

Words

1 _____ 2 _____

3 _____ 4 _____

5 _____

Trick Words

1 _____ 2 _____

Sentences

_1_

_2_

Unit Test Grading

Sounds: _____ / 5	Trick Words: _____ / 2	Score: _____	
Words: _____ / 5	Sentences:	x 4	
Marking: _____ / 5	Words: _____ / 5	Total Score: _____ / 100	
	Trick Words: _____ / 3		

☐ Legibility   ☐ Capitalization   ☐ Punctuation   ☐ Phrasing

Sounds

1   2

3   4

5

Words

1   2

3   4

5

Trick Words

1   2

Sentences

1 _____

_____

2 _____

_____

Unit Test Grading

Sounds: _____ / 5	Trick Words: _____ / 2	Score: _____
Words: _____ / 5	Sentences:	x 4
Marking: _____ / 5	Words: _____ / 5	Total Score: _____ / 100
	Trick Words: _____ / 3	

☐ Legibility   ☐ Capitalization   ☐ Punctuation   ☐ Phrasing

Sounds

1 _____   2 _____

3 _____   4 _____

5 _____

Words

1 _____   2 _____

3 _____   4 _____

5 _____

Trick Words

1 _____   2 _____

Sentences

1

2

Unit Test Grading				
Sounds: _____ / 5	Trick Words: _____ / 2		Score: _____	
Words: _____ / 5	Sentences:		x 4	
Marking: _____ / 5	Words: _____ / 5		Total Score: _____ / 100	
	Trick Words: _____ / 3			

☐ Legibility   ☐ Capitalization   ☐ Punctuation   ☐ Phrasing

Sounds

_____

- -

1   2

_____

_____

- -

3   4

_____

_____

- -

5

_____

Words

_____

- -

1   2

_____

_____

- -

3   4

_____

_____

- -

5

_____

Trick Words

_____

- -

1   2

_____

Sentences

1 _____

_____

2 _____

_____

Unit Test Grading			
Sounds: _____ / 5	Trick Words: _____ / 2	Score: _____	
Words: _____ / 5	Sentences:	x 4	
Marking: _____ / 5	Words: _____ / 5	Total Score: _____ / 100	
	Trick Words: _____ / 3		

☐ Legibility   ☐ Capitalization   ☐ Punctuation   ☐ Phrasing

NOTES

Capitalization and Punctuation

 Capital Letters

A B C D E F
G H I J K L
M N O P Q R S
T U V W X Y Z

 Capitalization

- Beginning of sentence: <u>T</u>he dog is cute.
- People's names: <u>J</u>ohn and <u>M</u>aria are here.
- Specific names of places: <u>L</u>ong <u>P</u>ond, <u>W</u>isconsin
- Days of the week, months of the year: <u>F</u>riday, <u>J</u>une
- Beginning word in quote: Mr. Smith said, "<u>Y</u>es, I will go!"

 Punctuation

- Period (**.**): I am six years old.
- Question Mark (**?**): When will you visit?
- Exclamation Point (**!**): I love this class!

Other:

- Comma (**,**): September 1, 2012
- Quotes (**" "**): She asked, "How are you?"

Mark My Words

Underline digraph

<u>sh</u>op   ba<u>th</u>

Underline each sound in a blend

<u>s</u><u>t</u>u<u>m</u><u>p</u>   <u>s</u><u>c</u><u>r</u>ap

Star the bonus letters

bal̊l⋆   puff⋆⋆

Box welded sounds

r|ing| h|am|

Underline baseword, circle suffix

<u>bug</u>(s)   <u>rent</u>(ing)   <u>publish</u>(es)   <u>hope</u>(ful)

Mark closed syllable   exception

c<u>ă</u>t
c

<u>wī</u>ld
d̸

Mark vowel-consonant-e syllable   exception

b<u>ā</u>ke̸
v-e

gĭve̸
v-e̸

Mark open syllable

n<u>ō</u>
o

b<u>ā</u> b<u>ȳ</u>
o   o

Mark r-controlled syllable

b<u>i(r)</u>d
r

c<u>a(r)</u>
r

Mark "D" syllable

pl<u>a(y)</u>
d

t<u>ea</u>m
d

Mark consonant-le syllable

bugle̸
-le

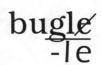

bubble̸
-le